Divine Healing + Divine Health = A Divine Life
The Three D's

EVANGELIST MARY F. SIMMONS

with Evangelist Bessie E. Breckenridge of Women of Faith
and Power Ministries, Inc.
http://womenoffaithandpowermi.injesus.com

authorHOUSE®

AuthorHouse™
1663 Liberty Drive
Bloomington, IN 47403
www.authorhouse.com
Phone: 1-800-839-8640

First published by AuthorHouse 12/31/2009

ISBN: 978-1-4490-6312-2 (e)
ISBN: 978-1-4490-6670-3 (sc)

Printed in the United States of America
Bloomington, Indiana

This book is printed on acid-free paper.

Contents

Special Thanks

Brother Anthony Reid for allowing the Lord to use him for this great and enduring vision via prison. You will be well rewarded along with your dear sweet mother, Evangelist Bessie E. Breckenridge, whom the Lord blessed me to have ordained in Ashtabula, Ohio with Pastor Deanna Hughes.

Acknowledgements

The people that the Lord allows me to meet and embrace daily is my source of love, joy and inspiration.

My Mother Susie M. Simmons, late granparents and dad has given no less than a thousand percent to my life. They have instilled, the true virtue of faith worketh by love and power, from my earliest existence through Godly discipline and wisdom.

Eugene, Jerome, Elizabeth and Darlene, my siblings has and continue to contribute much inspiration as well as challenges in my life to be all that God has ordained for me to be.

Introduction

The only qualifications that I posess is Godly inspired, and He anoints this servant to empower and educate His people to be all that He has made them to be in this present world.

We are living in a time, where health seems to be the number one priority. Health care is outrageous, and the hospitals have no choice but to shorten stays and find other ways and means to help us to recover at home. Nursing homes are filled to capacity with long waiting list, and they can't build them fast enough to keep up with demand.

Let's face it folks, we are living longer, but we are not healthy. We must return back to the garden of eden before it is too late. The garden of eating healthy....lot's of fruits and vegetables and not so much meat. Take in some oatmeal everyday...did you not know that oatmeal is one of the healthiest foods that one can consume. Oatmeal water is another form of eden and it will help us to be protected from colds, flu's and a lot of immune problems.

The time is now that we learn to practice the word of God......James declares, that we must not be hearers of the word, but doers. Our very lives depend on it. Remember, the first commandment God gave to Israel......Hear O Israel the Lord our God is one, and the second is this....faith cometh by hearing and hearing by the word of God. Our lives depends on our ability to hear what thus says the Lord and faith is the hand that supplies the word in healthy doses every day. If you can hear and follow directions you can live a long and healthy life just like the saints of old.

I am a product of faith, I practice what I preach and teach. The Lord can't and won't use me if I am not in good health....what kind of an example would I be? At the age of twenty-nine, I suffered a drastic illness, because of poor nutrition and the lack of proper rest. I started to stud nutrition in order to heal myself (Physician heal thyself). Jesus assures us that we can heal ourselves by following the holy scriptures. Our Patriach John.......III John 3......Beloved, I wish above all things that

thou mayest prosper and be in health, even as thy soul prospereth.........
the key is to walk in truth.

The Lord sent me three angels, Mother Neal, Mcghee, and Thompson. They brought me a product made out of pure herbs, namely KM. KM was the worst tasting liquid that I had ever encountered, however, the Lord allowed it to work and seventeen days later I was discharged from the hospital in the name of Jesus. I continue to use as many herbal products as the good Lord allows on a daily basis. Please note that herbs will not heal you, but rather taking them mixed with faith in the Almighty God will do the job.

I have had many other surges of illnesses and surgeries to cut out the disease, but they have been minor compared to what I have suffered in the past due to my lack of acknowledging the Almighty God. Now I seek him on a daily basis and my steps and diet is ordered by the Lord and not my own desires.

Studying herbal products along with the word of God will change your life. In chapter fourteen of Deuteronomy, you will find the dietary laws that God gave to the children of Israel, and we are the spiritual children of Israel, and what God says to one, He says to all. There were none that was sick, feeble, or full of diseases. Their diets was ordered by the Lord and our's should be no differnt, if we want to live a long healthy useful life in Christ.

Faith Speaks

For in Jesus Christ neither circumcision availeth anything, nor uncircumcision; but faith which worketh by love.... Ye did run well; who did hinder you that ye should not obey the truth?

Galatians 5:6-7....... Faith cannot and will not work if you are not walking in the truth, and I don't care how much faith you have, it will not work unless you are walking in love. Love is not lip service... it is action...it requires work. Apostle Paul spent a long time in I Corinthians 12-14 expounding on love....give it a shove and see what it does for you my friend.

Now faith is the substance of things hoped for, the evidence of things not seen....Hebrews 11:1. Substance....the very essence in your soul that brings about results. We cannot see faith, however, we can feel and be assured that it works. So then, faith cometh by hearing and hearing by the word of God. I love what Jesus said to Thomas, Blessed is he that believeth and has not seen. We donot need eyes to have faith, faith is simply taking God at His word and doing what He says.

As faith speaks (Jesus) listen and pay close attention and you will be truly blessed. Faith says, if thou canst believe all things are possible to him that believeth, and whatsoever you desire when you pray, believe that you receive them and you shall have them. Faith do not doubt nor wonder and it sure does not look back. Arm yourself in love and walk in love at all times and see what the Lord will do and bring to pass in your life. Sometimes, it is important to change our minds about somethings and get the very mind of God...Let this mind be in you which was in Christ Jesus......Jesus had a mind to please His Father in all things. If you love the Lord you will keep His commandments... St. John 14:15........and his commandments are not grievous...it will not harm you it can only bring about abundant life. Don't be a fighter or close minded....allow the Lord to open your mind so you can receive all that He has for you and your loved ones. Amen

Dedication

A debt of gratituted and thanksgiving to the one's that has contributed to the writing and the very life enhancing abilities, that has sustained me in gathering the information that you will find within these pages.

First and foremost, I thank the Almighty God for giving me the courage and grace to be able to organize my thoughts. Second, Evangelist Bessie Breckenridge, whom the Lord allowed her son, Anthony Reid, to be incarcerated for a short time in order to share a dream with him and present it to me, and it will unfold in this book.

Evangelist Breckenridge is truly a blessing to me, through her wonderful insight, she has assisted me in pulling this material together in more ways than she could ever imagine. May the Lord ever bless her and her son Tony.

Sarah Jane Taylor and Dale Davis for their thoughtfulness and guidance. Sarah has inspired me to write many wonderful things, and she is the one that ecouraged me to record a message entitled "Healing is yours for the asking."

Finally, to all that have encouraged me through the years, my friends, family, spiritual and natural. The House of God for instilling in me the true beauty of Holiness and the Commandments of the the Most High God. St. Matthew Baptist Church, Tillman, South Carolina, for showing me how to seek and to adore my Heavenly Father, and for allowing me to instruct them at a very early age, and for allowing me to represent them in the Sunday School Conventions. I shall never forget the debt that I owe them.

The Vision

Every one wants to be healthy. There are many man-made medicines, and there are many natural ones also: herbs, leaves, and roots which are called nature remedies. However, theyall prescribed by the great physician. before any of these things can work, there must be a cleansing. The body must be cleansed of all tokens and waste. We don't realize that most of the time our foods are not properly chewed, therefore, they cannot be properly digested and disposed of without the necessary help that the body and colon so badly need, and this is just the natural part. What about the spiritual....the heart must be clean and pure first.......Psalm 51:10...Create in me a clean heart and renew within me a right spirit. It is a wonderful thing to have a clean body, but it is just as important to have a clean and pure heart.

Accept God's medicine through obedience....keep His Holy Commandments, Statutes, Judgements, study His word, and meditate upon them day and night. Allow your inner man to be saturated with the word of God. Beleive that all things are possible.......Praise God, let His praises continually come from your mouth.

Good health is promised to the obedient ones. The scripture let's us know......Only believe...St. Mark 9:23; Call those things that are not, as though they were.....Romans 4:17 A merry heart doth good like a medicine....Proverbs 17:22. God sent His word and healed them...... Psalm 107:20; III John 2....Beloved I wish above all things, that you would prosper and be in health even as your soul prospers.

God spoke to me on the first day of the week, April 12, 1996. He told me that His people needed to be taught how to receive a healing and how to hold onto it.........Where there is no vision the people perish..... Proverbs 29:18. This vision is based totally on the word of God. The Lord went on to say, "I gave your founding father's....Bishop Johnson, Bishop Smith, andd Bishop Rawlings, the master plan, however, it is up to the believer's to pay close attention and follow so that the next generation might have faith and do the same. It must be practiced and heeded daily less we forget.

Divine Healing must be taught each time we come together, make mention of it, keep it in your spirit, let it not depart from you all the days of your life. This is an health law....forget them not, they must be kept strictly according too: Leviticus 11 and Deuteronomy 14. Know how your food is prepared, who is preparing it, and know how it was raised. The cattle and the swine must not be raised together. If they are raised together and living in the same pasture, they are contaminated together, therefore, they are unclean unto you, because the swine is unclean, and anything it touches becomes unclean unto you. Buy no beef, chicken, lamb, veal, turkey, venison, quails, or pheasants that have been in contact with pork products. Do not cook them together, or mix them in any way, they are unclean unto you.......do not buy them. Purchase no fish with fins and scales that have been touched by a cat fish it is contaminated. We must read labels carefully and do not eat animal fat. Products that contain animal fat can be anything. No what you are eating and buying. Purchase no jiffy products, no frozen or refrigerated pie crust or baked goods that say lard or animal fat........ you may purchase products that contain vegetable ingredients only.

God says, "My people perish for the lack of knowledge.....Hosea 4:6 The Lord further said "My people need to be taught how to be healed, and how to hold onto their healing." Healing is your's for the asking. Change your thinking and your life will follow.

Divine Health

The Bible promises salvation and healing for the sinner, yet health is also promised to the believer. (1). Sickness is not the will of God, but it is the will of the devil. (2). God made health a law and a statute. It is against Divine Law to be sick. (3). Some people in Bible days preserved there youth into old age. (4). Paul's thorn in the flesh was not sickness. (5). With two exceptions, there are little record of any Godly Bible saints being sick. The average saint who believes in "Divine Healing," takes for granted, that getting sick at least ocassionally. and getting healed, is God's order in their lives. Yet according to the scriptures, this is not "Divine Healing".............Divine Health which is God's intended plan for His children. This fact has been made so clear in the word of God that it seems impossible, that so many saints could make such a mistake. Notwithstanding, the sad truth is that the majority of believer's expect a certain amount of sickness, and consider this the normal.

In searching the old and new testament, I find that these two books agree on the subject, and reveals that "Divine Healing" is more or less an emergency measure, provided by the Lord in the event a child of God, through possible neglect of health laws, or some such case he may obtain deliverance from the Great Physician who is always the Lord that healeth thee....Exodus 15:26. Repeated illnesses should not be the normal experience of the new testament saint. The will of God for us is clearly expressed by the Apostle John......III John 2.......Beloved I desire above all things that thou mayest prosper and be in health as thy soul prospers. It is obvious, however, from this scripture, that health is not an unconditional blessing, but is inseparable associated with prosperity of the soul, as is indicated by the words "even as thy soul prospers".

To solve the problem of sickness which plagues so many saints, it is necessary to first make clear that repeated healings are not God's best for His people, rather His second best. As long as we live in the thought that we must get sick, though the Lord will heal us, and do not rather take dominion over sickness, refusing to tolerate it, it will forever be a menace to us. As long as we do not recognize sickness as a curse, as the work of satan, as something to be banished from our lives, we are likely from time to time fall into it's trap.

Divine Health originated in the Garden of Eden. God's will for His people in the Garden was health, and the same applies today. Man was made in the image of God, and therefore free from sickness. He possess a perfect physical body, although it was mortal, subject to death. Death is an enemy of the human race. Likewise is sickness, for it is incipient death. Although man was created mortal it was intended that he should ultimately be immortal. The tree of life was planted in the midst of the Garden, and it is apparent that if our first parents had resisted the temptation to disobey God's command, they would have at length been given the opportunity to have partaken of the tree of Life; and as a result, lived forever. In fact, after they fell, they were thrust out of the garden to guard against this very contingency.

The fall of Adam and Eve brought in it's wake a trail of woe (deep suffering and misfortune). sickness and pain. Man was eventually to turn back to the dust from whence he came. However, in the trip back to the dust he would suffer from all manner of pain and suffering, incapacitating diseases, physical deterioration of old age, and finally death. In contrast to this sad scenario, was the situation of Adam and Eve before their fall, where in the garden of paradise, they had enjoyed the glory of edenic youth, with never a worry nor a care.

Adam and Eve had divine health when they were in the garden of eden before the fall. Sickness came only as a result of sin. Hence redemption which redeems us from sin, redeems us also from the curse that follows sin sickness. A double cure for a double curse. Exodus 15:26....and said, if you will diligently give attention to the voice of the Lord thy God, and will give ear to His commandments, and keep all His statutes, I will put none of these diseases upon thee, which I have brought upon the egyptians, for I am the Lord, that healeth thee.

Divine healing is mentioned only once in the bible before the covenant of healing was given. This instance was the healing of Abimelech and his family....Genesis 20:17. God made provision for His people to be healed before the law was given. There is never a time, when God in His infinite mercy will not give healing. All you need to do is repent of your sins and cry out to Him (The Lord). His ears is open to the cry of His saints.

Our leaders, also has a responsibility to the people, just as Moses...... Exodus 15:25........James declares; Is any sick among you? Let him call for the elders of the church; and let them pray over him, anointing him with oil in the name of the Lord: And the prayer of faith shall save the sick, and the Lord shall raise him up; and if he have committed sins, they shall be forgiven....James 5:14-15........If you are in desperate need of deliverance, do not hesitate to cry out to the Lord. He hears those who call upon Him with all their heart as the prophet Jeremiah said......... Jeremiah 29:12-13. Then shall he call upon me, and you shall go and pray unto me, and I will give attention unto you. And ye shall seek me, and find me, when you shall search for me with all your heart......(1) You must be honest when you go to God. (2) You must seek Him with your whole heart. (mind). (3) Cleanse your mind of all wrong thoughts. (Find out what wrong thoughts are and deter from them at all times.

As Moses cried unto the Lord, the Lord answered him....Psalm 34:6. This poor (less than adequate) cried, and the Lord heard him, and saved him out of all his troubles. Think of Hezekiah, after the prophet Isaiah came to him and said unto him, thus saith the Lord set thine house in order; for thou shalt die, and not live. Then he turned his face to the wall, and prayed unto the Lord, saying, I beseech thee, O Lord, remember now how I have walked before thee in truth and with a perfect heart, and have done that which is good in thy sight. And Hezekiah wept sore. And it came to pass, before Isaiah was gone into the middle court, that the word of the Lord came to him saying, turn again, and tell Hezekiah the captain of my people, thus saith the Lord, the God of David thy Father, I have heard thy prayer, I have seen thy tears: Behold I will heal thee: on the third day thou shalt go up unto the House of the Lord; and I will add unto thy life fifteen years........II Kings 20:1-6.

Healing and health is in the atonement......For He made Him to be sin for us, who knew no sin; that we might be made the righteousness of God in Him..........II Corinthians 5:21. The atonement speaks of Christ's bearing the curse in our stead. He takes the sin upon Himself that is ours. In other words, He (Jesus) bears our sins upon the tree.

Therefore, sin brings about sickness, and sickness if it is not healed, it brings death. You don't have to die, but rather live a long and productive life in Christ. Christ bore our sicknesses...St Matthew 8:16-17. When the even was come, they brought unto Him many that were possessed with devils: and He cast out the spirits with His word, and healed all that were sick: That His word might be fulfilled, which was spoken by Isaiah the prophet, saying, Himself took on our infirmities, and bare our sicknesses; because Christ bore our sicknesses, we do not have to bear them........We donot have to bear sicknesses and diseases again unless we want to.

Divine healing and Divine health is associated with the atonement of Christ. He bore our sins and sicknesses, therefore, we need not bear them again. The promise of healing is more than a blessing that we may accept or leave alone....it is our's for the asking. When a person who has years of usefulness before them, becomes, for instance, a victim of cancer, and fails to claim the promise of deliverance, he is breaking a divine ordained law. The penalty is death....Romans 6:23. When a person is put in jail for a period of time for a petty misdemeanor he may feel that the penalty is severe. However, the penalty for failure to claim the promise of healing and health can result in pain and suffering, not to mention heavy expenses, loss of time, and even death long before one's time.

God wants and needs healthy men and women who can labor for Him, and give Him and honest days work. God is going to see if His people will take Him at His word, or whether they will give up when the test comes. God wants to know if you will give up when the test comes.......will they believe the symptoms more than His word or will they confess defeat instead of faith. If we are going to claim the privileges of divine healing and health, we may be sure that we will be thoroughly tested, however, if we take our stand upon the word of God, and resist the enemy, we will find God's promise true and that He will surely stand by, because God keeps His promises. Divine healing and health is not an optional benefit which we may accept or reject as we see fit, nevertheless, God made it a statute and an ordinance....He commands us to be well.

The Covenant Of Healing And Health

With every divine promise there are of necessity certain conditions. Some covenant of healing and health is conditional, and there are four conditions. (1) If you will deligently give ear to the voice of the Lord your God. (2) Do what is right in God's sight. (3) Pay attention to His Commandments (4) Keep all His Statutes....................These conditions are clear and need no explanation..........Jesus said, if any man will do His will he shall know of the doctrine....St John 7:17....................Don't be like Jonah and run away........................and will do that which is right in His sight, and then you will know if it is of God or man.

The bible declares, there is a way that seemeth right unto man but the end thereof is death. It is remarkable the number of people who will openly dispute direct commands of the sripture, simply because they are distasteful to them. It is one thing to do that which is right in the sight of God, and another to follow ones self, and be wrong. In those days there was no King in Israel: Every man did that which was right in his own eyes......... Judges 21:25...... He who would have divine health will make it a point to do those things which are pleasing in the sight of the Lord and not that which is according to his own will.....I John 3:22..... And will give ear to His commandments. The Lord, puts emphasis in repeating, and keep all His statutes. God is obviously seeking to get His point across to His people. You may find divine health and healing, only, if you are committed to His will. We know that His commandments are not grevious.....I John 5:3). It is, therefore,a sad scenario when many seek healing on cheaper terms.

The promise of divine health is indeed a serious matter for every saint to consider. Divine health is God's plan for His saints. God has given us His word that if we will obey His commandments, He will not permit none of the diseases to come upon us that He brought (permitted) to come upon the Egyptians.................And ye shall serve the Lord your God, and He shall bless thy bread, and thy water, and will take sickness away from the midst of thee..........Exodus 23:25...................... God has promised that if we serve Him, He will send His angels before us; He will bless our bread and our water and take sickness from our midst..........The Lord also says, in the mouth of two or three witnesses, shall every word be established.............II Corinthians 13:1.................For the third time God speaks to us concerning divine health...............And the Lord will take away from thee all sickness, and will put none of the evil diseases of Egypt, which thou know, upon thee; but will lay them upon all them that hate you.

Health is a blessing, sickness is a curse....................Sickness and disease comes as a result of disobedience to God. All diseases common to mankind are included. The bible teaches that sickness is a curse for disobedience, and healing is a blessing from the Lord. Let us not be misled into making of non effect the plain statements of the word of our God...............If we fully obey the Lord our God and carefully follow all His commandments that He prescribes for us this day, the Lord our God will set us high above all nations on the earth. All these blessings will come upon us and accompany us if we obey the Lord our God................According to I Samuel 15:22...............And Samuel said, hath the Lord as great delight in burnt offerings and sacrifices, as in obeying the voice of the Lord? Behold, to obey is better than sacrifice, and to hearken than the fat of rams.

We as the children of God must be very careful to follow as dear little children, and obey in all things. Obedience is the key to receiving the blessings of The Almighty. We must obey them that have rule over us. In our daily walk with the Lord we must examine ourselves daily to make sure that we are obedient in all things. For if we are not careful to obey in all things, we will receive the curses of this Holy Book. There must be total surrender to God from the heart, not from the lips......out of the heart of man proceeds the issues of life. Don't be afraid to go back to Psalm 51 and repent of your sins, we must stop our foolishness. Repentenance means to stop sinning at once. The most important part of any saints life is to live free from sin. Practice living free from sin every day.....................Beloved I wish above all things that thou may prosper and be in health even as thy soul prospers............III John 2.

Do you believe healing works?

Psalm 105:37...............Yahweh brought them forth also with silver and gold: and there was not one feeble person among their tribes.

- There was no feeble ones

- They had no doctors
- They had no emergency rooms or hospitals
- There was no drug stores
- There was no crutches, canes , wheel chairs, no artifical limbs, or transplants (a few had staffs)
- There was no disease, illnesses or sickness, they were all in perfect health

Note: They had no diseases, illnesses, or sicknesses until they became disobedient to God.

Examples of Divine Health

And Moses swore on that day, saying, surely the land where thy feet have trodden shall be thine inheritance, and thy children's forever, because thou hast wholly followed the Lord thy God. And now, behold the Lord has kept me alive, as He said, these forty and five years, even since the Lord spoke this word unto Moses, while the children of Israel wandered in the wilderness: As yet I am as strong this day four score and five years old...(85 years old). As yet I am strong this day as I was in the day that Moses sent me: as my strength was then, even so is my strength now, for war, both to go out, and to come in..............this is the testimony of Caleb at eighty five years young. (1) Caleb was one of the spies who brought back a positive report. (2) He declared his faith in God (3) Entered the land when directed by God (4) God Gave him divine health. It is not God's will for us to deteriorate, become senile, incapacitated (incapable of functioning), mentally or physically.................With long life will God satisfy him and show him His salvation.........Psalm 91:16

What Did Yahweh Do For Moseh (Moses)?

Moses is called the liberator of the Jews, for the Bible tells us that he led them from slavery in Egypt to the Promised Land in Palestine. He was a great law-giver who gave God's people the rules (Ten Commandments) that have guided them and millions of other people for the last 3,100 years. It is believed Moses wrote the first five books of the Old Testament, which is also called the Pentateuch and the Books of Moses. The Book of Exodus, the second in the Bible, tells the story of Moses. He was born in Egypt at a time when the Egyptians were treating the Jews very cruelly. The Pharoah (King) of Egypt was afraid there was getting to be too many people, so he passed a law saying that all Israelites male children were to be killed. At this time Moses was only three months old. His mother, whose name was Jochebed, put him in a basket in the Nile River, hoping he would not be found and killed. Moses was found by an Egyptian princess. She pitied him and took him home. By chance, she asked Jochebed, Moses' own mother, to care for him.

When Moses grew up to be a young man, he heard a voice coming from a burning bush. He recognized it as the voice of God, and it told Moses that he would free his people from slavery. Moses could not speak without stammering, and he thought this would prevent him from being a forceful leader. But God appointed Aaron, Moses' brother, to be Moses' helper. He would speak for Moses, whose stammering made talking before an audience difficult. They went to Pharoah and demanded in the name of the Lord that the Israelites be set free. Pharoah refused. Then God sent nine plaques, or misfortunes, to Egypt, but still Pharoah refused to let Israel go. Then, in the tenth plaque, God killed the oldest male child in every Egyptian house but He passed over (spared) the houses of the Israelites, and this is told about in the Passover services.

Now Pharoah was very much afraid, and he let the Israelites leave Egypt. Moses led them out of the hated country. Then Pharoah was sorry that he had been so frightened and sent Egyptian soldiers out after their former slaves. Moses guided his people across the Red Sea, whose waters rolled aside to let them through. When the Egyptians followed, the waters rolled back, and the Egyptians were drowned.

Moses and his people stopped at Mount Sinai. Moses went alone up the mountain. God appeared to him there. To Moses, God renewed the covenant, or promise, that He made to Abraham and the nation of Israel. Then the Lord gave Moses the Ten Commandments and between them were the Statutes and Judgements. They were written on stone tablets. When Moses went down from Sanai, he found the people worshipping an idol, a golden calf. In anger, he broke the tablets which contained the Ten Commandments, Statutes (Feast Days) and Judgements (Righteous Rules and Regulations). But he made a great sacrifice, and offered himself to the Lord to make up for the sins of the people. The Lord spared Moses. After a year at Sinai, Moses commanded the people to follow him again.

Moses was the great law-giver that God used to present the law to Israel. Before Moses there were many systems of law, but none lasted very long. The Mosiac law has never been weakened since the time of Moses. It has been the foundation on which the laws of all great religions of the Western world have been built. Christians and Mohammedans, as well as Jews, still honor its principles.

Moses lived during times of average longevity of people was about the same as it is today.............seventy years. God added fifty years to Moseh's life...............And Moses was an hundred and twenty years old when he died: His eyes was not dim, nor his natural force abated (decreased or lessened). Everything was in perfect working condition...........Deut. 34:7.........This is more than divine health, this is divine life.........Exodus 28-33.............When Moseh came down from the mount, his face shined with celestial glory.

There are also celestial bodies, and bodies terrestrial: but the glory of celestial is one, and the glory of the terrestrial is another...............I Corinthians 15:40. (1) celestial is devinely good; of the heavenly; godly, holy, perfect, ideal or exquisite. (2) terrestrial.......earth or earthy, inhabitants of the earth, wordly, mortal or human.

The New Testament And Health

We have seen and heard that the Old Testament goes beyond healing to Divine Health. It is significant that we find none of the leading disciples sick. There was, of course, sickness in the New Testament Church, however, it was not something that was commended. Apostle Shaul (Paul) considered it an indication of something amiss (something wrong).

For he that eats and drinks unworthily, eats and drinks damnation to himself, not discerning the Lord's body. For this cause many are weak and sickly among you, and many sleep. (A) Discern---discover with the eyes and mind (B) It represents the Blood of Jesus Christ (C) The Blood of Jesus was shed for us (D) We must take communion according to knowledge not zeal....Romans 10:2.........The body of Jesus was broken for us............St. John 19. ....Jesus allowed His body to be broken in order to keep ours from being broken. Jesus has already borne our sickness. We need to discern (know) what God has done for us.............wake up and know in whom you believe and why you believe!

It is important at the communion hour that each believer know that the water (cup) represents the Blood of Jesus that was shed for you and I.....It was the Bloood of Jesus, and it remains unto this day a cleansing for our sins. The bread that we break, represents the Body of Jesus Christ, that was broken for us, and instead of us, so that we would be whole. This cup is the Blood that was shed in the New Testament, we must teach it to all of God's people so that they can understand fully. Leaders must tell the good news and make sure that each saint knows the redemption story! The Body of Jesus was broken so that our body could remain whole.

We are members of the mystical body of Christ. Mystical means spiritual (relating to direct communion with God). There is a physical body of Christ. Saints are members of this mystical body of Christ.

And wheter one member suffers, all members suffer with it; or one member is honored, all members rejoice with it.....I Cor. 12:26

A schism between members of the body of Christ can result in sickness in the whole body. (A) schism=split   (B) We must examine ourselves to see if we are in the faith and have Godly relationships with one another. Saints are members of the spiritual body of Christ. We should have care one to another or we will ourselves suffer. Christ's body never had sickness while on earth. Since we are now members of His body, we should not be sick.

Health And Prosperity

Keys to success in Health and prosperity.

- III John 2
- St. Luke 13:16
- Acts 10:38
- St. John 5:6

Do you want to be made whole_____

Know this...........sick believers are of little help or benefit to the Kingdom of God...............Divine Health is not for the careless, or for the disobedient, or for those who seek His blessing for purely selfish purposes. If you are not prospering in your soul, do not expect Divine Health in your bodies, because both must go together, just like faith worketh by love.........Genesis 4:7 and Galatians 5:6............A sick soul invites a sick body..............you donot want leaness of a soul to creep in.

The New Testament teaches Divine Healing and health. John the Apostle desires above all things that the believers prosper and be in health, but only as their souls prospers. Failure to prosper in one's soul could well jeopardize the health of one's body.....Remember, that you do not have a soul....you are a soul (nephesh) a living soul.

There has been so many false accounts of Apostle Shaul's (Paul's) thorn in the flesh. Some say it was his eyes, marked by pus; other say, it was many things, but what they say doesn't matter, however, what really matters is what does God say. What they say has no basis or foundation unless it is proven by the word of God. The Bible says to prove all things....I Thes. 5:21.......Hold fast to that which is good. We shall see in the sriptures that in every case. the term thorn in the flesh is used to indicate persecution by wicked people and not diseases.......Numbers 33:55; Joshua 23:13; Judges 2:3. We further see in the scriptures (Old Tetament) A thorn in your side or in your flesh is not a disease, but rather it is a personality whom the evil one uses to annly (annoy=disturb or to irritate) or even on occassion persecute us, the children of God.

Notice.................St. Matthew 5:11.................we must allow scripture to interpret scripture then the matter will be forever settled........ Psalm 119:89. There is no place in the Bible where Paul says that he is blind or sick. In every passage of scripture where Paul speaks of his thorn in the flesh, he refers to it as an infirmity or infirmities............II Cor. 12:10..............necessities, persecutions, and distresses. In the previous chapter eleven he names twenty-three infirmities and distresses................ Ii Cor. 11:23-33. Let us not be found saying again, what they say, but rather be in agreement with the Word of God. We must study to show ourselves approved unto God, a workman that needs not to be ashame, rightly dividing the word of truth.........II Timothy 2:15.

Apostle Paul labored.................Can a sick person labor?.........I Cor. 15:10. We may suffer from infirmities and distresses and yes persecutions, however, we need not suffer from diseases.................... Phillipians 2:26-27 and verse 30....This man put his health in danger, so he could help others..................Epaphroditus had depleted his nervous energy, and as a result became gravely ill.....................We sometimes take on too much, therefore, our bodies need rest for an extended period of time in order to have health restored. Even in our infirmities, distresses, and persecutions it is only for a season.........I Peter 5:10.

Give God Praises and Glory!!!!!!!!!!!!!!!!!!!!!!!!!!!!! What you have heard and seen do!!!!!!!!!!!!!!!!!!!!!!!!!!!!!! Great is the Lord and greatly is He to be Praised. Give the Lord the Highest Praise. Do you know in whom you believe?_____. When you have Divine Healing + Divine Health you have a Divine Life...............Go tell every body that you have A Divine Life in Christ...........Yahshua The Messiah......Shout Glory!!!!!!!!!!!!!!!! Come on and give Yahweh praises and glory!!!!!!!!!!! God is not keeping you sick..........you are allowing the devil to keep you sick.................You can have what you say............ Romans 4:17..............and I am saying that I have Divine Health from the Divine Healer and He has given me a gift of Divine Life.

Does Healing Work

It depends on you. Right and wrong thinking plays a tremendous role. Many cultures thrive on negativity...they believe what they want to with no Biblical basis to prove anything, they just fly by the seat of their pants. Right thinking is the only way to achieve A Divine Life. This thinking is based on the pure unadulterated word of the Living God undiluted from the Original King James Version which is the pure word of God. In this Bible, the word of God is pure and written by Holy men as they were inspired by the Lord (Yahweh). Change your mind about the old wives tales...... generational curses will be reversed through the word of God.

Your mind.....Apostle Paul admonishes us to let this mind be in us which was in Christ Jesus.....Phil. 2:5. What kind of mind did Jesus have? A mind to please His Father and believe me, we need the same mind to please our Heavenly Father............with this natural mind, we cannot please God because flesh is an enemy to God. The mind or the brain controls the whole body and it is extremely important that we learn how to protect and take care of it at all times. What we think affects our whole being. The brain can be healed and controlled by our physical activities, such as our diet, exercise and mood. As we study the word of God it is important to understand why God gave His people Israel a special diet, and we are apart of Israel, we are their descendants through Abraham, and it is important that we know and realize that we must except the rules and regulations of the Most High God if we want to live a long and productive life and continue to prosper and be in health. Remeber, you cannot prosper unless you are in good health.

As a people we have been fed a lie from our earliest existence by false teachers concerning our diets. The one thing that I encounter as I travel across the country is that pork is the other white meat. This is a lie from the pits of hell and I will tell you why. "Of their flesh shall ye not eat."....Leviticus 11:8.

This meat is marketed as the other white meat and millions of people are eating it inspite of the warnings from the word of God. Even health care providers have warned it causes strokes, high blood pressure and other illnesses to be uncontrollable. God has always had a dietary law for His people..........Deut. 14 and Leviticus 11.

Before man was placed in the Garden of Eden, God had formualted a dietary formula for him to enjoy which insured that he and his descendants (who we are) would live forever. God said, Behold, I have given you every herb bearing seed, which is upon the face of all the earth, and every tree, in which is the fruit of a yielding seed; to you it shall be for meat.........Genesis 1:29. Here in this plan we will not find any flesh therein, yet man eats pork (swine's flesh) regularly inspite of the danger and warnings.

Centuries ago after creation, Noah and his sons left the ark to discover that the flood had destroyed vegetation from the earth. God allowed them to enjoy certain types of clean meats......Genesis 9:3. Every moving creature that liveth shall be meat for you, is limited to beef, chicken, turkeys, lamb, goat, veal, quails, fish, with both fins and scales, venison, ox, hart, pheasant and some others in Palestine or Jerusalem...........Leviticus 11 and Deut, 14. Before Noah and his family went into the ark, God told them how to make a distinction between the clean and unclean animals, therefore, Noah knew the truth concerning the dietary laws before hand.

The word of God clearly speaks of every clean beast thou shalt take to thee by seven, the male and his female: and of beast that are not clean by two, the male and his female; to keep seed alive upon the face of all the earth..........Genesis 7:23. Only an all seeing, knowing God could forsee the damage the flood would cause on vegetation, therefore, He planned for man's need in advance by perserving the clean animals, so that they could replenish and provide food for the people.

If just one hog had been slaughtered, sickness, illnesses and death would have been ramparted upon the earth, because of disobedience to God's master plan. Many today, (professing Christians) believes that this law is only for the Jews. This is the farthest thing from the truth. When you come into the knowledge of the truth and accepts Jesus Christ as your Lord and Saviour, then you are as He is A Jew............ Spiritual and Natural. Why, because He changes your very nature. We are one in Christ Jesus diet and all............think about it.

God has placed the swine (hog, pig) in the same catergory as the rat...........Isaiah 66:17. The swine is full of demons which causes it to be contemptible. Even legion knew the swine's were unclean and he asked the Lord to cast the demons out of him into the swines......St Mark 5:1-19. God's purpose for creating the hog is for it to be a garbage collector...........he is nothing but a scavenger. Whatever he eats goes throughout the body, therefore, when you eat it, it becomes a part of you..........unclean.

As a young person, I was raised on a farm, personally witnessing the filthtiness of the pigs and hogs as they would wallow in the mud, lying and rooting on top of a manure pile with his head buried in the mess exalted in his highest filthy glory for all to see. One writer states in II Peter 2:22, but it is happened unto them according to the true proverb,,,,,,The dog is returned to his own vomit again; and the sow that was washed to her wallowing in the mire.

Farmers realize how important it is to have hogs, because once the cattle is in the barn, the hogs are let out to eat the waste so the hogs become fat for the market, and you go, buy it and digest all that mess. Isn't this enough to make you sick? Have you ever tried to put lipstick on a pig, fight a skunk, or raid a buzzard's nest while wearing perfume?

Hogs will eat anything including their own babies and all other dead stinking animals. Remember all of these diseases are digested by the hog and when you eat pork chops, chiterlings, bacon, ham, ribs and any part of the pig oh yes hot dogs, you are digesting exactly what it ate..........and you ask why am I dying with this incurable disease? Shame on you!

Swine (hogs, pigs) was designed to be scavengers, to eat up filth, therefore they are an a abomination; however, when finish doing there jobs, it was not appointed to mankind to eat such filth. Some have even tried to compare the hog to the chicken. There is a vast difference between the hog and the chicken. First of all, the chicken has two stomach's, the glandular stomach and the gizzard with a double skin which is easily separated. The hog has but one stomach.

Did you realize the animals that chews the cud and divides the hoof, such as the ox, sheep, goat, deer, buffalo, and the cow; because of the saculated condition of the alimentary canal and the secondary cud receptacle, have practically three stomachs, as refining agencies and cleansing laboratories, for the purifying of their food; thus weeding out from their systems most of the poisonous and deleterious matter.

It takes clean vegetation food over twenty-four hours to be turned into flesh. Have you ever thought about foods that are not vegetation, how many hours does it take to turn into healthy nutrition for your body to digest?

Yes, healing does work as long as we follow as dear children the plan He has outlined and left on record for us even today. If you must eat unclean foods, it would be just like Eve, when she took that famous walk in the Garden of Eden and met the snake who totally confused her, and she ate of the trre, and brought some to her husband and from that day forward it has been death, because of disobedience. We cannot afford to put unclean meats into our system and expect God to heal us.

The saints of old as well as today, knows how important it is to follow God's instruction to the letter. Commandment Keepers, Jewish, Israelites, Muslims, Seventh Day Adventist, Temple of Yahweh and many other's know the importance of the dietary laws............they have A Divine Life.......why don't you be obedient and live. Do you think Naaman would have recovered from leprosy had he been disobedient to God's dietary laws? Know what you are putting in your mouth.

The Human Brain

The brain is the most powerful organ in the body......it can be trained and developed to do whatever we program it to do or be with the proper nutrition. Many have invited healing into their bodies, by changing what they ate and thought. We can use the mind to bring about total restoration with the word of God. Before man was created God planned his diet so he could live forever, but because of disobedience, he brought life to himself and all his descendants. However, God sent His son Jesus to restore mankind back to life, if man would only believe, repent, be baptized in th name of the Lord Jesus Christ, and he shall recieve the Holy Ghost speaking in other tongues as the Spirit of God gives utterance.

Our brain requires natural stimualtions not chemicals, drugs, alcohol, vast amounts of caffiene and other poisons which will destroy it over a prolong period of time. We can help our brain to improve by eliminating posions from our bodies. Our brain should function as a well oiled machine and it will purr like a kitten. The way to do this is detox....yes detox....get rid of everything by cleansing your colon and do not return to bad habits. Change your habits and change your life.....Be a conniseur of learning, never stop learning new and challenging things, add fish oil to your diet every day. Certain types of fish is better than others. Salmon, sardines, and tuna along with trout are leaders among the seafood giants. Shrimps, lobster, squid, and other shell sea foods are scavenger's just like the hog and they were not made to be consumed by human beings...they bring about diseases and eventually death.

Exercise is one of the greatest things you can do for your life after cleaning up your diet. All forms of exercise is good, however, some are giants in helping you to get blood flowing to your brain and other vital organs so you will feel better, do better and begin to enjoy your life. Dancing is not only great exercise it will boost your immune system and stimulate your brain function. I really know that some saints don't believe in dancing, unless they are under the influence of the Holy Ghost, but when last have you danced for the Lord. I love the Jamaican Saints, they will grab a holt of you and give you a whirl around the floor and a Glory Hallelujah time will be had by all..............so why not go ballroom dancing, or polka dancing or square dancing and I .... yes, I can assure you that God will not punish you...He may just have a little fun at your expense...He does have a sense of humor. We need to do something at least twice a week or more to get our heart rate up......Another good source of exercise is sex, for those who are maried regardless to age or physical ability......it will surely change your mood and improve your endorfins.

Social connections is a premium for our brain, therefore, clubs, church, outings, fishing, skiing, golf, table tennis and the like is important even though you make not want to participate you can watch and cheer on your favorites as they improve their quality of life and at the same time your can boost your immune systems by enjoying the competition.

Positive thinking is one of the great ways to boost everything, by planning your future with interesting things to do with your mate, friends or family. It creates excitement just by thinking about the possibilities of things to come your way. Show some gratitude........focus on what you love about your life and the things that you are grateful for each day and make notes in a journal to share with other's, and don't just be in the group, be a force in the group...bring ideas....challenge them to be all that they have been designed to be without worrying about what other's might say or think. Learn how to be yourself...get in touch with your inner self.

Prepare a shopping list....don't just go to the market and purchase the same old things......buy things that are healthy and that will improve your memory, sex appeal and stamina.............like green teas, blueberries, walnuts, broccoli, salmon, tuna, oatmeal, avocado's, red bell peppers, spinach and turkey products. After all you want to improve yourself and get rid of the old boring, unfocused you. Learn to smile and laugh more....no one enjoys being aroud an old foggy person. Endeavor to drink more water, try some oatmeal water it will help you to prevent the common colds, flu's and other little maladies. It was said that one winter in one of the coldest cities in the country, all the men was given oatmeal water due to the fact they were working outside in the sewer and railroads and even some were prisoner's and none of them got sick. Oatmeal is one of the best things that we can put into our bodies.

Always avoid alcohol, cigarettes, second hand smoke. Have good ventalation when using house hold products and when you visit a beauty shop or salon that uses chemical. These things all will go into your brain and cause problems over an extended period of time. Be careful with dyes, your hair is turning gray for a purpose, and if God wanted us to have black hair all of our lives, he would have designed it that way. Whatever, we put on or in our bodies, eventually will got to the brain through our blood streams.

Personal Testimony

It is important to recognize here and now, that the Lord will heal us if we do that which is pleasing in His sight, however, we must follow the instructions that He has left here on earth for us. It is important to stay with the dietary laws, exercise and avoid all scavengers. The more weight one gains the more medications your doctors will prescribe, so if you keep your weight down and eat in moderation, you will find, your life and conditions will improve automatically and you will be able to eliminate certain or all medications as the Lord begins to restore everything in your body to normal. The Lord will not over power anyone to bring about changes in your life. We have heard for centuries........if you make one step the Lord will make two, this is is not scriptural, however, we must be determined to improve our life and the Lord will aide us in becoming all that we desire....we have to be willing to submit and do the things that are pleasing unto Him.

I was naturally sickly from birth and my parents and grand parents sought the Lord and He told them what to do in order for me to be healed. Then as I grew older sin crept in, and the Lord sent His Holy Word and healed me. Many infirmities had plaqued my body, however, none was able to hold onto me for long periods of times. Allow me to give you a list of things that I have experienced in my life.

- I Peter 5:10 assures me that afflictions will come, however, they come for a purpose, and I have experienced them all.

- Heart attack...............less than six months on medication............ the Lord showed me which herbs to use for this problem and today I have a healthy heart.

- Nasty ulcers......after long intense medical treatments, even at Cleveland Clinic, nothing worked, so once again, God used herbs to heal me.

- Right knee placement.........:....the Lord blessed me to conquer this by His Holy Word.

- Back Injury...................the Lord showed me to use herbs to bring relief until He blessed me to find a surgeon to remove the diseased part.

- Infirmities and persecutions have brought about much stress, inspite of it all, I've learned how to lean and depend on the Lord.

- A ruptured pattellar tendon, I thought for sure would have knocked me off my stool, yet the Lord blessed me to find another surgeon to perform surgery and correct the problem many surgeries later, physical therapy, nursing home stays, the love of friends and family and many long lonely nights wondering when will I be able to walk again without help. Today, I am healed by the grace of God. I only need to use a cane for support, but, my greatest support comes from the lord....He is my Divine Healer.

- Time and chance happens to us all, just as time is creating havoc with me, it is not leaving anyone behind, that is why it is so important to pay attention to word of God and His people who have gone on before us. Mark the perfect and upright man for at the end of that man or woman is peace. Hebrews 12:1-2, Psalm 37:37

- Satan comes to kill, steal and destroy, God comes that we should have life and that more abundantly.

Many suffer from generational curses, they too can be broken and overcame by the blood of the Lamb. All it takes is a change of attitude and direction in the word of God. We must denounce those things that are not like the Lord. What our fore parents practiced before our arrival on the scene, really doesn't have anything to do with us, unless we decide to follow in their foot steps. Joshua said to the people..... choose you this day, whom you will serve, as for me and my house, we will serve the Lord. It is a conscious decision to live or to die.

The Lord gave our founding father's a master plan, however, it is up to us to follow it and teach it to our children throughout their generation. Divine healing must be taught each time we come together..........make mention of it...........put it in your spirit........let it not depart from you all the days of your life

Health Laws

Forget them not, they must be kept very strictly

- Know how your food is prepared
- How it is raised
- By whom they are prepared
- The cattle and the swine must not be raised together
- Buy no beef, chicken, lamb or veal that is near pork.
- Buy no clean fish that is close to catfish
- Cat fish has a monthly cycle just as a female and it has no fins or scales.
- Read labels very carefully... .....do not eat animal fat products.......
  an animal could be anything (examples are Jello products, Jiffy and Pie Crust...make sure you know what is in these products before you purchase them.)
- Rise Peter kill and eat has nothing to do with food............yet it has everything to do with people of other faith's coming to except the truth of the Lord.
- Everything that the Lord has made is good and nothing to be refused.....to them that know the truth. If you know the truth, you know that everything that the Lord made was good for something. The question remains, is it good for you?
- Sometimes it maybe difficult to convince your family members, concerning certain foods, because they will tell you..we have been eating this all of our lives and it hasn't killed us yet. Consider this, what about diabetes, high blood pressure, , high cholesterol and the like. Have you ever considered, that if you didn't eat scavenger's, would I be suffering with this disease. We hold the power of life and death in our hands......which will you choose?
- Those things that was against us was nailed to the cross. What things.......that was against us....The blood sacrifices, killing of

those poor little innocent animals every year just to cover our sins.

- Divers washing, burnt offerings, the scape goat, peace offerings, the offering for a sin offering through ignorance, the trespass offering for sins done deliberately, meat offering, offering at the consecration of a priest, the purification laws, leprosy, middle wall of petition that prevented women from coming into the temple for worship......all of those laws that had to be performed daily, weekly, monthly and yearly..

- The dietary laws was never against us, they are for our good..... donot drink any blood or eat any fat.

- The life of the animal is in the blood.

- Study the word of God for yourself and find out, waht is right and what is wrong....

- It is not up to your Pastor to tell you everything, especially the truth if He or She doesn't know it........II Timothy 2:15; St. John 5:39.

The time has arrived for all of us to know the Lord for ourselves from the least to the greatest. This is not the time to ask.....do you know the Lord.

Note: Try using sea salt rather than regular........you will use less.

A To Z

- Attitude....................posture or relative position, feeling, opinion or mood

- Behavior...................the way that one behaves, or the act of behaving

- Character.................trait or distinctive combination of traits, peculiar people.

- Diet............................food and drink spiritually and naturally

- Energy.....................capacity for endurance

- Earnest....................serious state of mind

- Faith.........................taking God at His word without questioning, belief and trust in God.

- Genuine...................never changing..realness

- Habits.......................usual behavior practiced

- Ignorance...............lacking knowledge, unaware

- Jolly.........................something said or done to provoke laughter, we need laughter

- Kindness..................essential quailty (tender hearted)

- Love...........................strong affection, enjoy greatly

- Management.............control....temperance

- Moderation...............avoiding extremes

- Natural.........................not artificial....simple and sincere

- Obedience................willing to obey

- Pride............................being pleased

- Esteem.........................think not to highly of ones self.

- Quietness..................not loud (peaceful)

- Rest..............................relax, resist, find a quiet place to meditate

- Sanctify......................think holy

- Secret Place..............where no one but you can go

- Truthful......................do not lie to one's self

- Thoughts...................must be pure

- Understand...............know what you are saying and doing

- Variety.......................collection of different things

- Works.........................keep oneself busy

- X-ray...........................self-examination (take a look deep inside of yourself

- Yearning...................tender or urgent desire

- Zeal............................enthusiasm (be enthusiastic)

We must be healed body, mind, soul and spirit.

Herbs and there uses for today

Aloe XL Juice............ .is made from certified whole leaf barbadensis gel that is made with proprietary process which removes the undesirable aloin and aloe emodin, but protects the two hundred and fifty plus nutrients found in the plant. This product is a non-concentrate with no water added. The result is a blend that maximizes the availability of vitamins, minerals, amino acids, enzymes, polysaccharides, and other various nutrients. Aloe XL juices contains at least 7000 mps which exceeds standards set by the International Aloe Science Council. This MPS count nearly triples the quality of our closest competitor. Aloe XL acts as a natural anti-inflammatory agent, penetrates all layers of tissue, helps to relieve pain associated with rheumatoid and osteoarthritis, which is an anti-bacterial antiviral, and fungicidal. This product help with gastrintestinal conditions such as ulcers, hiatal hernias, and irritable bowel. It is topically used to relieve psoriasis, eczema and acme. It is one of the world"s most potent immune system boosters. This product is also being tested with AIDS and cancer research, and it contains important digestive enzymes. It can help to regulate cholesterol and triglyceride levels, and stimulates cell division three fold.

Aloe XL Juice can be purchased in a variety of flavors: such as Strawberry Kiwi, Orange Papaya, Cranberry and Pennsylvania Peach...........each product contains....the following herbs: Pau D' Arco, Ginko Biloba, Enchinea and Ginger Root.

Aloe XL Liniment......contains the combination of an anti-inflammarory with an analgesic, and it is five times the strength of your current aloe liniment product.

Aloe XL Creme.......a natural cleansing, moisturizing, and healing agent. Used in combination with the aloe natural to help treat eczema and psoriasis.

Aloe XL Gel........a therapeutic healing agent that acts as an antibacterial, antiviral, and fungicidal treatment. Used in combination with aloe natural to help with treat acne and shingles.

Aloe XL Derm....an aloe gel containing a wide variety of healing enzymes which helps to expedite the topical healing process.

Black Walnut........oxygenates the blood, burns up excessive toxins and fatty materials, helps balance sugar levels, breaks down cystic tissue. Instead of dying your hair with chemicals, use the water after boiling to rinse and leave in your hair...........also good for intestinal problems in children as well as adults.

Blueberries.........diabetes

Bladderwrack.....helps normalize the thyroid gland and aids in combating obesity.

Boron....may play a role in helping to prevent osteoporosis and help your brain work better. This herb appears to have the essential minerals necessary to prevent bone loss.

Burdock---good for lower back pain

Chromium....stimulates metabolism of glucose for energy.

Cat's Claw........maybe beneficial in the treatment of cancer, arthritis, allergies, systematic candida, chronic fatigue syndrome.

Dandelion.....used to increase the flow of urine, and is slightly laxative.

Elderberry...........uses the leaves after boiling for a poultice to soothe hemorrhoids with a little olive oil.

Fennel...all kinds..helps with obesity, appetite control and reducing flesh and other internal problems

Ginger Root.....breaks down protein and reduces cholesterol, aid digestion

Gotu Kola....may help improve memory, has a calming effect on the body, good expectorant

Hawthorne Berries......improves blood flow, may lower blood pressure

Indian Hemp.......excellent for breaking up colds, and influenza..... stops hiccoughs...good to stimulate growth of hair

Jersey Tea (Red root)......spleen trouble

Kerosene......scalds and burns

Licorice.....reduces pain from ulcers, reduces pain and stiffness from arthritis, may help retard growth of certain cancerous tumors.

Ma Huang.....known to increase stamina and vitality, is known to increase metabolic rate and burn calories, also a powerful bronchial decongestant.

Nutmeg.......indigestion and gas

Oatmeal......prevent illnesses and lowers cholesterol (water is excellent for immune system).

Papain.....derived from papaya, helps break down protein, improves digestion, reduces the need for antacids.

Querctin....several studies suggest that this herb maybe a potent cancer fighter, also prevents the release of histamine, thus inhibiting the allergic response, maybe useful against asthma.

Resveratrol........an anti-fungal compound in grape skins that lowers fat content in the liver, thus lowering overall cholesterol and protecting against heart disease.

Sea Salt........use it for gargles and nostrils to keep viruses,colds and flu at bay twice a day...Your doctor does!

Stealth Free...........is a caffeine free product that utilizes natural extracts to give you that extra boost of energy when you need it too boost metabolism and helps to promote appetite control.

Tumeric...is a natural anti-inflammatory, may also prevent heart disease, prevents the formation of dangerous blood clots.

Turpentine..........place it in a saucer under your bed or child's when a fever is near or to cure one.

Uva Ursi.....womb troubles

Valerian.....good for epilepsy

Wild cherry bark------excellent for phlegm in throat

Xanthoxylum......(Prickly Ash)............a wonderful tonic and stimulant

Yarrow Root.........helps to improve appetite in older adults

Zwieback...........A wonderful bread source during difficult times.

In Bible times they used to combine different grains and legumes and make them into bread. "Take thou also unto thee wheat, and barley, beans, lentils, millet and fitches, and put them in one vessel, and make thee bread thereof..........Ezekeil 4:9.

Healthy Recipe☐s

Prosperous Salad
Shreded Coconut
Fresh pineapple........chopped
Apple juice
Chopped red delicious apples
Fresh Mango....chopped
One teaspoon cinnamon
One teaspoon ginger
Mandarin Oranges
One tablespoon rum extract

Mix all ingredients together, chill and serve after one hour in refrigerator. Contents depend on family and serving size.........Enjoy in moderation

Pottage Stew

One venison roast cubed, placed in half apple cider vinegar and water to cover over night in refrigerator. Next morning take meat out of water and rinse throughly. Place a little olive oil, chopped onions, red bell peppers, garlic cloves in hot pot and sautee all ingredients until golden brown, add meat, beef broth and cook until tender. Add meat is tender, add potatoes, carrots, celery and season to taste.

Lima Bean Soup

One package of dry lima beans

Sock overnight in enough water to cover

In the morning pour the water off the beans and rinse once more

Place the beans covered with water in a soup pot with smoked turkey parts

Cover and cook on medium heat for 45 minutes

Add red bell peppers and a can of tomatoes

Season to taste with a little cumin, tumeric, sea salt and cayenne pepper

Southern Corn Bread

Old fashioned corn bread mix about 2 cups

1 cup lite soy milk

1/4 cup butter

1 large egg beaten

A pinch of nutmeg

Bake bread for 35 minutes or until golden brown.......great with lima bean soup, you can also add a little lima beans or any other beans or peas to the mixture before baking.

Venison El Primo

Wash or rinse meat in cold water

Place in dish, pour enough buttermilk over meat to cover

Place in refrigerator overnight

Next morning remove meat from refrigerator, rinse throughly

Season as desired

Place on hot grill and cook until done

This meat can be broiled, baked or fried

Best Ever Chicken Wings

12 wings or more depending on your family size

Bud lite beer to cover wings in refrigerator over night

Take out of refrigerator, add seasoning

Paprika

Sea Salt

2 tsp cumin

1 tsp ground garlic powder

1tsp marjoam

2 Tbs. olive oil

Preheat oven to 425 degrees

In small bowl, mix cumin, garlic, marjoram, paprika and salt.

Use another small bowl for olive oil, and mix chicken in it first

Rub spice mixture over chicken

Pour a little olive oil onto large baking sheet, spreading wings a little apart so they can evenly bake

Bake for 25 minutes.

Turn them over and bake for and additional 25 minutes until slightly crisp and golden brown

Serve hot with your favorite sauce or as is.

Home made sausages

1lb ground chicken

1lb ground veal

1 tsp sea salt

1 tsp cayenne pepper

2 Tbs Sage

1 tsp marjoam

1 Tbs chopped garlic

1 large onion chopped finely

1 tsp honey

2 Tsp olive oil

Mix all ingredients well in a large bowl

Shape mixture individually into small sausage patties

Place on a tray for storage in freezer

Place the trays in freezer bags and place one in th freezer and the other in the refrigerator for breakfast etc.

Stuffed Veal Breast (Grass Fed is best)

   2 lbs veal breast

   6 slices beef bacon

   3 slices bread, toasted and cubed

   1/4 lite soy milk

   1 egg beaten

   1/2 lb ground chicken

   1 small onion chopped

   1 tbs chopped garlic

   1 teaspoon sea salt

   1/4 tsp cayenne pepper

   1/4 tsp sage

   1/4 tsp tumeric

   Pace egg into a small bowl, whip until smooth and creamy

   Add all other ingredients into bowl with egg.

   Toss in bread crumbs

   Rub meat inside and out with olive oil, salt and a little pepper

   Take mixture, place inside of the veal breast and wrap the beef bacon around the veal breat

   Add a little water in pan before putting in the oven

   Place in roasting pan in a 350 degree oven for 45 minutes, check after 45 minutes to see if it is cook to your desire.

Veal Fricassee (Grass Fed Meats are better)

   2 lbs 1/2 to 3/4 inch veal steaks

   Salt and pepper to taste

   2 Tbs enriched flour

   1 teaspoon tumeric

   1 cup lite sour cream

   1/2 cup beef stock or a little water added to beef stock

1/2 chopped onion

1tsp chopped garlic

2 Tbs olive oil

Place flour, salt, pepper, tumeric in bowl

Place Olive oil in pan on top of stove, pan should be sizzling hot, when you place meat

Place veal in one at a time in mixture, coating both sides evenly

Place in hot mixture, one at a time until pan is full

Reduce heat to medium, cover and let cook

Turn them after seven minutes or cooked to your desire

Add onions, and garlic along with your liquid (beef stock water mixture)

Continu cooking for an additional 20 to 30 minutes on medium heat.

Adjust heat according to your needs.

Healthy Tips

I have found when eating fruits out of a jar it is more flavorful to add a little ground ginger and cinnamon. This mixture is excellent for people that have diabetes. Cinnamon helps to regulate blood sugar. Ginger tea from the root is great for indigestion and there maybe some benefits to using it to help with other infirmities.

Ginger powder and the liquid from roots can be used to make breads and other desserts.

Cattle that are fed grass are better and lower in fat than grain fed beef and they deliver more nutrients.

Take a note from the Chinese............eat more rice, it is high in carbs.....especially brown rice or wild

Add peanuts to entrees to help you stay satisfied longer.

Peanut butter and jelly is still a great food source and filling with a glass of lite soy milk.

Use honey to sweeten teas and coffee to liven up your beverages.

Drink plenty of water and other non decaffinated beverages to keep yourself hydrated.

Always find ways to bring laughter into your life. Laughter is good for your health.

Don't practice spending long periods of time alone, it leads to lonliness and depression.

Learn to experience different cultures, food, dance and expand your horizon.

Find some projects to work on, challenge yourself in writing, painting, collages and the great out doors.

Don't let life pass you by..........nvite the Son in and experience all the benefits He has to offer you.

Sing and rejoice openly with gusto and zeal and allow us to enjoy our differnces.

Don't dwell on your disability.............Dwell on your abilities.

It is better to lose at love, than to never have loved at all.............take a chance, you might be surprised.

Give love a push, it may just stick around for life.

Life is a peach my friends...let's enjoy some before it is all gone.

Conclusion

Divine Healing + Divine Health = A Divine Life has been a pleasure to write and share with you. I hope that you will embrace all that the Lord has for you and your family. Don't be afraid, shy or embarass to ask for what you want, take it by force if necessary. Life is too short to settle for anything less.

We are living in a time where all things are possible despite the economy. The economy has nothing to do with, the blessings of the Lord. Lift up your eyes to the hills from whence cometh your help, with your hands lifted, a mouthful of praises and a heart filled with thanksgiving and bless the Lord. All the blessings are still right here on this earth, the Lord has not removed nothing, all that is needed is a little faith to capture your right seed to obtain your harvest.

Continue to walk with the King (Jesus) and be a blessing and know that your deliverance is right around the corner if you do not give up.

Special Thanks

To my church family, and Jonathan Dillard for encouraging me to continue along the path where the Lord has led me and to continue to be a blessing to all people and share the talents, abilities and gifts that He has blessed me with.

To my sister Liz, who encouraged me to hold onto my passion for writing and walk in the path of righteousness all the days of my life.

Final thoughts: I eat to live. Why? Because, I enjoy eating lots of great tasting foods that guarantees favorable readings as far as cholesterol is concerned with freedom from heart disease, protection from cancer, and maintain my youthful vitality into my later years. I have learned that good health is our greatest wealth. This is why you ought to "Eat To Live."

Reverse Diseases through Nutritional Excellence. We think that we know so much about nutrition and its a powerful fact to create disease or protect against disease. However, the question remains unanswered by the masses of our population as to what constitutes a healthy diet that does actually protect us rather than harm us. What will reverse diseases once it has invaded human beings. The Almighty God left a diet for all mankind...........Leviticus 11 and Deuteronomy 14.

We must change our brain and then our life will follow..........Let this mind that was in Christ be in you... ....Pysician heal thyself.

Epiloque: Bishop Alexander Ravenel, II

It really comes down to how we feel about ourselves. How do you feel, think, and see yourself? Maybe you do not believe God cares enough about you to want you to be in good health. Do you feel that God wants you to be in good health? Can you imagine God, who controls all that He created you to be in poor health? God formed us from His precious good and perfect earth............Genesis 1:26-27.............We are as He is.

After God created us in His image and likeness, we became a living soul. Soul is God breathed, "the divine source of all identity and individuality." The divine source. which is distinct from our physical bodies.

A'saph in Psalm 82:6...............God in him, through him and as him says, "I have said, Ye are gods; and all of us are children of the Most High." Man (the human-----being without refernce to sex) is God.........Genesis 6:5-7.

Now if we are gods as the scriptures declares............we are made in the image and likeness of Almighty God. Then is not God (our soul) grieved at the wickedness we do to our bodies along with the evil imaginations of our hearts? Through programming we have and do continue to destroy our bodies. What? Know ye not that your body is the temple of God? Our bodies was given to us so that we may function on this great and perfect earth

Was not our Patriachs, and Matriachs programmed to destroy themselves? Why do we continue in their ways? Know ye not that our bodies are the members of Christ..............I Corinthians 6:15. Christ represents the expressed mind of God. He is expressed by Jesus, the Messiah. Yahshua represents the expression of God in us, through His Son. Therefore, we must change our thinking and be not conformed to this world by the renewing of our minds in Christ Jesus.

Live food for a live body equals life.   Dead food for a live body equals death.   Slow, but sure.   Dead food for a live body equals sicknesses and diseases.   Think about this!   Can we bind rotten and bonded material together for a proper garment?   How many times does man and the earth have to be destroyed before we get it right?

Consider the foods you consume.   Where does it come from?   How was it prepared for your consumption?   Does it contain any elements that alters your thoughts causing you to not walk in the righteousness of God to the very point of destroying your body?   Take stock and repent. Repent, that is..................I Corinthians 6...........do something different even if you think that you are in perfectly good health and everything is going well.

Stop and study what goes into your body.   I know that there are many obstacles to the bottom line...............not with God.   The Lord will direct you in your dietary needs..................only listen and obey. Practice what thus saith the Lord and He will heal and restore your body to maximum health so you can be about your Father's business and do His purpose for your life.   Don't be paralyzed to think that you do not know what God's purpose for your life is.   You can start with Ecclesiastes 12:13-14.

There is no need to be ignorant...............You need not be lost................. What has been written in this book and what you have read only need be heeded.   Give attention.   Hear.   Keep.....Do.....For your own sake..... Will you?

I leave you with Romans 12:2

Thank you Evangelist Mary F. Simmons for the many churches (Healthy bodies) that will be raised because of your submission that God may express Himself through you...................May God bless you all to be a blessing to yourselves.

Resources:

The Holy Bible

Dr. Mehmet Oz,   Dr. Joel Fuhrman...................Eat To Live

Change Your Brain, Change Your Life...............Dr. Amen

Back To Eden..Jethro Kloss

How Can I Use Herbs In My Daily Life?.............Isabel Shiphard

Other Books by: Evangelist Mary F. Simmons

Why the swan sings

Sarah's Story

The Old Woman and the River

Why the swan echoes and a complete series on
the swan coming soon.

Ministerial Tapes, DVD's & CD's

Women of Faith and Power Ministries, Inc..........First Anniversary
    Dinner

Educational Messages

Radio Broadcasts

Valuable Info........In time of Need

If Thou Canst Believe

History of Church

Faith Without Works Is Dead

Be Content

A Calendar Comparison

Mutt & Jeff

WFPM'S Vision

WFPM Luncheon

New Home

Question & Answers

In The Time Of Trouble

Help From Hidden Hands

Out Of Prison To Reign

Who Is The Holy Soirit

Set The Captives Free........6 tape series (A treasure in a box)

Doctrine Of Spiritual Gifts

A Two Kind Of Love

Why The Swan Sings Series

Faith Worketh By Love

Unfulfilled

Sabbath Morning Sacrifice

My Praise For His Glory

Behold How Good

The Prayers Of The Forgiven with Poetry & Poems

From Clutter To Contentment

When Grace Has You In His Grip

Creatures Clean & Unclean

A Designated Diet

Healing Is Yours For the Asking

Other Ministerial Resources will be coming with next publication along with free gifts with your purchases.

You may write to me @ Womenoffaithandpower@yahoo.com with questions or comments.

Updates will be posted on our website @womenoffaithandpowermi. injesus.com

Evangelist Simmons is a well re-nowned speaker, Prophet, writer, author and a friend to countless. She has traveled far and wide to bring the redemption message to many and continues to witness to great and small everyday. The Evangelist was ordained in 1985 in the House of God, she has one son, Philip Q. and countless recordings, plays and other fine works of love and devotion to her Lord......................She is a "Tramp for her Lord"!

Evangelist Mary F. Simmons is Founder and Chairman of Women of Faith and Power Ministries, Inc., with affiliation nationally and internationally.

Manufactured By: RR Donnelley
Breinigsville, PA USA
February, 2011